A YELLOW ROSE IN THORN'S CLOTHING

BY
LANA LEE

Copyright © 2024

All rights reserved.

A Yellow Rose In Thorn's Clothing

TABLE OF CONTENTS

ACKNOWLEDGEMENT 1

AUTHOR'S NOTE 2

ABOUT THE AUTHOR 3

ME 4

DAD (1959-1968) 5

WAYNE (1969-1971) 14

STEP DAD #2 (1974-1977) 23

MAKING THE BREAK (1976-1977) 34

HUSBAND #1 (1977-1979) 38

NEW BEGINNINGS (1979-1982) 48

FROM BAPTIST TO BARS (1982-1984) 57

HUSBAND #2 (1984-1987) 69

LIFE AT RURAL INSURANCE (1987-1996) 89

MOVING ON (1996) 114

A Yellow Rose In Thorn's Clothing

ACKNOWLEDGEMENT

I want to give special thanks to the people who inspired and supported me through this process: My maternal grandparents and great aunt - Earl and Velma Intolubbe and Cepha Intolubbe Jesse, who wrote their own brief memoirs for all of us grandchildren to read and appreciate, Amber Darwin – a good friend and author of adult / dark fantasy / paranormal romance books, Rebecca "Reece" Lummus – my initial editor and cheerleader of my story, posthumously Jaimie Sherling – my Mary Kay rep, friend, musical performer and author who managed to write two books in three years before metastatic breast cancer took her in 2023, to all of my friends who believed in me, and of course Bellevue Publishing for making this dream a reality.

AUTHOR'S NOTE

I intend this book to be one of two, the first half of my story. The one where some people apparently believe that in the end, I rode off into the sunset with a blonde-haired, blue-eyed successful businessman who "saved my ass." Except that, there is much more to my story, and the ending isn't exactly looking like a fairytale. That will be in book two. This book will explore my life up to, and somewhat after, meeting my third husband. I suppose he did save my ass in some respects, but it wasn't exactly a free ride. I've hardly laid under a palm tree on the beach in the shade, swinging in a hammock, eating Bon Bons and grapes fed to me by humble servants. Please, this is my actual life we're talking about. No one I know, no matter how good they have it, lives a life like that. So, come along with me. Cry for the sad times, laugh at the good times, throw pillows at the TV if you get angry enough. Most importantly, I hope you can relate, empathize, sympathize, and try to understand. I am far from perfect, and I'm willing to admit it. Try not to judge me too harshly.

ABOUT THE AUTHOR

I am a 65 year old widow living in Madison, Wisconsin. I am the mother of two grown children, step-mother of two and grandmother of seven grandsons and one granddaughter. I have spent almost twenty years putting this first story together, and am in the process of writing a second one. After the loss of my husband in October 2023, from Lewy Body Dementia, I have spent a lot of time recovering, remembering and writing. I am an ordinary person who has faced challenges and overcome them, faced disappointment and risen above it. My hope is that this story will resonate with other ordinary people who think no one understands what they have been through or are going through. My goal is to provide inspiration and strength to anyone who has dealt with difficulty in their life, and prove that you can overcome anything if you just believe in yourself and never give up

ME

My Mom said they brought me home from Shepard Air Force Base Hospital during a Texas dust storm. I was born on Wednesday, March 11, 1959. Interestingly, there was another Laura Howell born on the same day in the same hospital. Maybe we were switched at birth. Except I think she was black and I don't know what her middle name was. My Dad named me Laura Louise.

DAD
(1959-1968)

My Dad served in four branches of military service – Army, Navy, Marines, and Air Force. I'm not sure in what order, except that he retired from the Air Force. I didn't see him much, as he volunteered to serve in Vietnam. My Mom divorced him when I was about eight years old. I always thought he was a "Tex Sergeant" because he lived in Texas. I realized much later that he was a Tech Sergeant. He was also an alcoholic.

I don't remember that much about Dad. It seems he served (voluntarily) in Vietnam most of the time my parents were together after I was born. We lived in a trailer home in my Granny's backyard. She had persimmon trees, honeysuckle vines, and a dog. She watched my sister and me (mostly me, as Carolyn was 5 ½ years older) after school. She was already somewhat elderly as my dad was the youngest of eight kids. Her husband, my grandpa, had died when I was two, in a sanitarium, from alcoholism. I remember watching Ben Casey on TV in her living room.

One day, my Granny came to our trailer for a late lunch or early dinner. My sister had not yet come home from school. My Mom and Dad got into a big fight about it. Mom was crying and going through one Kleenex after another. Granny jumped in and told her that maybe Dad wouldn't be so mad if Mom would stop throwing her snot rags on his plate.

I remember my dad singing a funny song to me one day in the car. I don't know if there was more to it, but what I remember is, "She's got freckles on her butt, she's pretty." I was young, but I caught the innuendo.

Besides Vietnam, Dad didn't move around after I was born, except for the year we lived in El Paso. I wasn't in school yet, so it must have been 1963-1964. Kindergarten wasn't required in those days, so I didn't start a formal education until first grade. By then, we were back in a trailer home in Granny's backyard.

While living in El Paso, I made friends with a girl a year older than me, Sharon Daugherty. I decided to walk from our trailer to hers (yep, we were still in a trailer) on a very hot summer day with no shoes on. By the time I got there, I had huge blisters across the bottom pads of my feet just below my toe line. I have a picture of us on another warm day, standing in a puddle with summer clothes on and me with a fuzzy winter cap. Guess I was a bit of a weirdo even then.

At least once (I don't remember if it was more than that), we all piled in the car and drove across the border to Mexico so Dad could get tequila. I guess it was cheaper there. I was being goofy and said I was going to hide on the back floorboard, but my mom said no because the border patrol might think we were up to something.

The last time I saw my dad after the divorce, I was sitting on his lap in a chair in the living room of our run-down duplex. He had tears running down his face. I was eight. Other than his mother's funeral (my Granny), where he showed up drunk, I didn't see him again until I was eighteen.

My sister and I spent the summer of our parents' divorce with our maternal grandparents in Concho, Oklahoma. Our Mom told us about the split over the phone.

I have to interject a section on our maternal grandparents, Earl and Velma Intolubbe. They were very supportive of my mom and of us. They lived in Concho, Oklahoma, which was close enough for us to spend holidays and summers with them until they retired and moved to a cabin they had built at Lake Texoma.

My grandparents worked at the Concho Demonstration School, a small boarding school for Indian students they established and helped construct. Grandpa was the superintendent, and Grandma was his secretary, and "Girl Friday," as she put it. She would let me use her typewriter and I wrote a few stories one peck at a time. I still have one of those typewritten stories, "The Spies Who Loved Horses." Who knows, it may still get published someday.

I remember some students walking around with Tarantulas on their shirts (okay, maybe one student; I was STILL very young). We were also able to watch some baby birds hatch in a nest that the parents had built in the outside corner of a window in one of the buildings.

Grandma was very good at crafts, and Grandpa was an accomplished watercolor artist. They both encouraged the grandchildren to pursue artistic endeavors and instilled a deep sense of pride in us, as Grandpa was half Choctaw Indian, which made each of us one-eighth.

My grandparents had a piano, and I would pick out songs by ear. I also composed some songs of my own, but they are long lost now. The first thing I remember ever wanting to be was a concert pianist. I realize now I never would have had the discipline to accomplish that. I had a lot of other aspirations, singing, private detective, and something practical, accounting. The last one is what I succeeded the most at, but not to the extent I hoped I would. Periodically I wrote poetry and over the years I would be commended for my general writing skills. I tossed around different story ideas, but never took it very seriously. I kept hearing "write what you know." What did I know better than my own life? So here I am, publishing my first book, an effort nearly twenty years in the making.

While school work and other things came relatively easily to me, I never felt like I accomplished anything significant. The important things were always a struggle. If it hadn't been for my third husband, I would probably feel like a complete failure.

I don't remember my grandma being angry with me herself, per se. I remember getting in trouble for turning the spigot on to the water thermos on a family picnic and not being able to turn it off, so all the water drained out. Everyone was mad at me then. I also locked myself in my grandparent's bathroom, and Grandpa had to climb in through the window to get me out. I got a spanking for that one. So maybe it was a subconscious act that my entire family, including some of my cousins, once left me at the Oklahoma City Zoo.

One of the kids piped up in the car, "Where's Laura?" I was sitting on a bench somewhere inside, just waiting for someone to come get me. My own personal version of "Home Alone" long before the movies came out.

A Catholic family lived on the other side of the driveway from my grandparents. I believe after the last kid was born, there were twelve children altogether (literally boy, girl, boy, girl all the way down the line). I was good friends with one of the younger daughters, Rita, and I had a huge crush on one of her brothers, Gary. I was only seven, and he was probably ten, so he had zero interest in me at all. My grandparents had a good-sized porch on one side of their house. I would stand out there and pretend I was singing to Gary, "Don't Talk to Strangers Baby" by Sonny and Cher.

My Dad never wanted my mom to work or have a driver's license. While he was in Vietnam, she took correspondence courses in secretarial skills, including shorthand. Eventually, she got a job with Merrill Lynch, which provided the necessary income for her to leave him. She still didn't have a driver's license, but we got by with public transportation and help from friends until she met the man who would become my first step dad.

Our first living quarters as a single-parent family were in a rundown, roach-infested duplex across the street from a city park. The city would water the park until it was pure mud. One day, I put a sign on the fence that said, "Please stop watering. This is a park, not a lake," or something to that effect. Remember, I was eight.

A little comic relief here. While living in the duplex, I surprised Mom (we called her Mama back then) by doing the dishes before she got home from work. She was so pleased that when she got home the next day, I said, "Mama, I did the dishes again, and this time I used hot water and soap."

I met one of my best friends in first or second grade. We had this very serious discussion about which was worse, losing your dad because he died, like hers, or losing your dad because of divorce. I don't know that we came up with a good answer, it was a conversation that two eight-year-olds shouldn't have been having in the first place. That was fifty-four years ago, and we are still really good friends.

My Mom, grandma, and, eventually, my sister were accomplished seamstresses. My second-grade teacher took me around to all of the other classes to show off a dress Mom had made that had a cat appliqued on the front. I wore the same dress in second grade, minus the cat, when I was chosen to parade back and forth across the stage as The Yellow Rose of Texas while the rest of the class sang the song at one of the PTA meetings.

While I was in fourth ~~and fifth~~ grade, we moved out of the duplex and rented a house right across the street from my grade school, Sam Houston Elementary. It was much nicer than the duplex, and I could walk to school. Carolyn went to Wichita Falls High School, "Old High" for short. I don't remember how my sister got to school, and she didn't get a driver's license until she was eighteen.

WAYNE
(1969-1971)

I don't even remember how my mom met Wayne, I think it was a blind date. He was overweight and not physically attractive, but he convinced her he was a good Methodist Christian. Church was always very important to my mom; she was a good person. She just had poor taste in men. So much for "Women tend to marry men like their fathers." My grandfather was an icon in my life. He and my grandmother were not just religious but true Christians. They weren't perfect, but who knows how I would have turned out without their influence in my life.

Wayne helped my mom get her driver's license. They got married, and we moved to a different school district. In fact, I didn't even go to the school in that district because we carpooled with a woman who took my sister to high school, so I went to the grade school right next to it, Hirschi High School and Kate Burgess Elementary, where I went for 5th and 6th grade.

During their two-year marriage, my Mom could afford braces and glasses for me. At first, I thought glasses were cool, but I always hated wearing braces, as if I didn't have enough going against me. My orthodontist was kind of weird, and braces in those days were very painful to get on or tighten, so I hated him, too. At least I was skinny until 7th grade when I got my period and instantly put on twenty pounds. It's been an uphill battle ever since.

Turns out Wayne was a closet alcoholic and a complete asshole. The two years they were married were when my grades fell. I went to sleep at night, listening to him yell at her for taking her showers at night and other ridiculous arguments. We had at least two TVs, one in the living room and one in their bedroom. Once, he made me change the channel on the living room set, so I went into their bedroom to continue whatever I'd been watching. He was not happy about that. He would get mad that the throw rug under the coffee table wasn't straight. He told me once that I caused all of the static around the house (because he obviously had nothing to do with it). He hoarded silver dollars; he had bags of them.

During this time, my Mom taught me how to read music. Bless her soul, she listened to me pick out one note at a time until I could start putting simple music together.

My sister was sixteen, and being that I was eleven and at the age where everything she did was cool, I wanted in on it. She was constantly annoyed by me getting into her clothes and makeup. She would hand me down 45s sometimes, though, and I had my own record player to listen to them on. You know, the kind with little yellow plastic pieces to keep the records on the turntable. Well, if you don't, you're too young to read this story anyway. Carolyn was into The Beatles and Jimi Hendrix. I was into The Monkees and Bread; close enough.

We had our sisterly fights, but we were probably the closest we would ever be during those two years, taking a stand together against Wayne. One day, who knows where the parents were, we took off on a lark and walked for what seemed like forever (could very well have been 3 miles one-way) to a little shopping mall. Those were the days of large hoop earrings, psychedelic colors, and polka dots. As I mentioned earlier, my sister was a proficient seamstress, so she would hem her skirts up, and Mom would let them out. Rinse and repeat.

My best friend in those years was Martha. Ironically, we were introduced by the daughter, who was one grade behind us, of one of Mom's co-workers at Merrill Lynch. Neither of us was really friends with her after that. Martha had a great Dad, but her stepmom was a bitch, so we commiserated together. We were both reading the book Harriet The Spy. Our teacher was a kook (must have been sixth grade). When I got busted writing notes about my classmates (and her) as Harriet did, she wanted me to come up and write them on the blackboard until she read what I wrote. Closed that case pretty quickly.

The homeroom was the art room, where we sat at big drawing tables. One day, while "Mrs. Kook" (I think her real name was Mrs. Keck) was out of the room, I decided to start jumping off the tables. Of course, I got busted for that, too. She asked for my parents' telephone number. I saw her put it on her desk, and as soon as she left the room, I grabbed it and disposed of it. She forgot all about it and never asked me for it again. My sister graduated from high school and got married to a blue-collar alcoholic asshole. Even worse than our dad. They moved to Ft. Worth.

My Mom divorced Wayne the summer after I finished 6th grade. We were able to move back into the house on Miami Street, where we lived before she married him. We were supposed to get a dog, a sweet, goofy-looking Mut. The house had a fenced-in backyard, and the owner had three dogs, so she was going to give us one. Before we moved in, someone, I think it was one of the neighbors who didn't like the dog, had it put down. We got an ugly, obnoxious Chihuahua instead named Teensy. Ugh.

While we lived in that house the second time, my sister had her first child, my nephew ~~David~~. We would go visit them in Ft. Worth. I loved becoming an aunt at the age of fourteen.

We moved out of that house, and I begged and pleaded with my mom to stay in my sister's old high school district. She wouldn't make me any promises, but we ended up moving into a "duplex" of sorts within walking distance of my junior high school, Zundelowitz, or "Zundy" for short. When I say "of sorts," my mom and I lived in a good-sized house, and behind it was a smaller one that was also rented out.

One day someone called while I was home alone and wanted me to give a message to the tenant out back. I walked back and knocked on the door. I don't think I was imagining it when he answered the door nude. I shoved the note at him and hauled ass back to the house. I wasn't a bad kid at all, but those two years were some of the most challenging yet.

We didn't have a shower, and I hated baths, so once, while my grandmother was visiting, my mom and I got into a huge fight because I refused to take a bath. She and Grandma were crying, but I was thirteen and stubborn and won that round.

Also, back in the dark ages of my youth, combination locks were not as common as they are now; at least, I didn't have one. I had an old-fashioned key lock. We had been to visit one of Mom's best friends, and somehow, my keychain with my school lock key got left at their house. I walked to school the next morning and panicked when I couldn't find my key. So, I walked back home without telling anyone. A while later, the phone started ringing. I wouldn't answer the phone because I told my mom later that it sounded "angry." After hearing from the school that I hadn't shown up and attempting several times to reach me by phone at home, Mom finally CAME home. We got my keys back, and all was forgiven.

Slowly I started to friend the kids who lived across the street. I got my first kiss from a brother, Dale, who was one grade ahead of me. I think it came as a dare from his older sisters. In high school, he became a big football jock, and he wouldn't have acknowledged me to save his life.

I was supposed to have gone to bed one night, and so was my mom. The kids across the street were laughing and having a good time so I snuck out my bedroom window and went to join them. Our phone rang, and I could hear it across the street since it was summer and the windows were open. My Mom got up to answer it and I scrambled to get back in through the window, but not soon enough. Yep, BUSTED again.

Another day, I was innocently messing around and decided to do a flip on my bed, which was right next to a closed windowpane. My feet hit the window and shattered it. Mom was less than enthusiastic about that but took it well. We cleaned up the glass and she even commented that some unexpected money showed up to pay for the new window. Whew.

Last but not least, a school friend from grade school came over to spend the night. My Mom was cooking something in the oven, roast or turkey or maybe ham. It created a light wave of smoke coming out the front door. Kelly and I had gone to the grocery store up the street and bought a pack of cigarettes for 55 cents. We sat on the railing outside my bedroom and smoked next to the front door. Miraculously, we did not get caught that time. I didn't smoke another cigarette until I was about twenty-three years old.

When I started high school in 1973, we moved to a house right across the street from it, renting from a gay male couple. They were super nice and great landlords. Despite our religious Methodist background, my mom didn't seem to consider it. Good for her.

I got my braces off just in time for my freshman class photo. Looking back, I was cuter than I gave myself credit for. The next two years of class photos were not flattering at all, but I redeemed myself my senior year, even though Mom was mad at me for taking my glasses off. Other than slightly chubby cheeks, I thought it was my best school photo ever.

STEP DAD #2
(1974-1977)

Mom took up square dancing, and reluctantly, I went along. It ended up being a lot of fun and possibly the last time my generation had a decent participation rate in that particular club. That's where my mom met my second stepdad. Hey, he wasn't an alcoholic, and he was a good Methodist. Except he was a mentally ill sexual pervert. It was his best-kept secret. Things were improving.

When I was sixteen, Mom and Warren got married on March 31, 1975. The next day was April Fool's, so everyone thought it was a joke when I told them. It was the worst April Fool joke ever, and I didn't even know half of it yet. Along with a new stepdad, I inherited a step-sister who was five months younger than me. We were in the same grade but at rival high schools. Even though we lived in the opposite district, I got permission to continue in A

Capella Choir and the drill team. I got good grades. I had good friends. We lived in a nice house. Mom seemed happy.

I seemed to set the example for my step-sister. Everything I wanted, my stepdad insisted she had the same thing. I mean, identical. I picked out an outfit for Christmas, and she got the exact same outfit in a different color. I picked out a necklace; she got the same necklace but in silver, while mine was gold. It did not help with our already competitive situation. I wanted piano lessons but never got them because Cindy would have had to have them, too. It wasn't her, it was him. Probably his guilt complex over molesting her from a young child, which I did not know about until after I moved out of the house. Interestingly, he stopped having sex at all with my mom a few years after they were married.

Our parents were not the most supportive regarding getting our driver's licenses. I looked like an idiot when I took Driver's Ed, which was still offered through school at that time. We did get our licenses though, somewhere between sixteen and seventeen years old.

Initially, we took turns driving my Mom's AMC Hornet to school, even though Cindy was within walking distance of hers. I get it; share and share alike. On the weeks Cindy had the car, Warren drove me to school in his Little Brownie's Cookie van, which, based on the following events, became extremely uncomfortable until I got my own car, an AMC Gremlin, and a job at the Wichita Falls State Hospital working in the kitchen.

I turned seventeen, and we were out of school for summer break. I liked sleeping in, but I was up playing the piano, still wearing my pajamas and a robe. Warren came in the back door from his cookie deliveries for his lunch break. He pulled me up from the piano bench and started talking. The only thing I remember him saying was, "I want you to know what boys are going to try to do to you," as he slid one hand into my underwear and the other one up inside my pajama top. At first, I was too stunned to move. Then I pulled away and bolted for my bedroom and locked the door.

He never tried anything with me again after that, but my mom noticed I avoided him at every opportunity. Months later, she asked me what was wrong, and I told her. Her response was, "I'm sure he had good intentions." After that, I wasn't very close to my mom for a long time.

Despite everything, I still got pretty good grades in school. I made Alto Section Leader in A Cappella choir (which was a joke but still flattering) and also an ensemble called "Old High Singers."

The only thing I was ever very good at in the gym was archery. I loved our gym teacher, and one day, she told me I just needed to be more aggressive in volleyball. So, in the next set, I went after the ball, and so did she. We collided, and she fell on the floor. At first, I thought she was laughing, but she was seriously hurt. She recovered, and I tried out for the drill team. I think I made it because she didn't want me playing volleyball anymore. I wasn't great at drill team; no matter how hard I exercised, I couldn't kick worth a shit. I got a uniform, performed at basketball and football games, and never had to play volleyball again. Then we got a new gym teacher, and we didn't get along. Gym wasn't required my senior year so I dropped off the drill team.

My step-sister was also in the A Capella choir and on the drill team for the rival high school. I was the one who had to walk out of our house in enemy territory in my rival school outfits.

I was able to secure a somewhat coveted position as Teacher's Aide to my former biology teacher, Mr. Coffman, who, more girls than not most likely, thought was pretty hot. In fact, he later married one of his former students and it seems it worked out very well. I believe they ended up having three sons. I was sad to find out Mr. Coffman passed away just a few years ago.

In my junior year, I had an English teacher from hell, Mr. Davis. For some reason he seemed to have it in for me. I got Bs in conduct (does that even exist on report cards anymore?) because the girl in front of me kept turning around and talking to me. He and I were not meant to get along together. The only way I could transfer out of his class was to go to an accelerated English class.

I was good at English but I was in over my head. I loved Mrs. Clapp but got Cs in her class despite my best efforts. My fault, not hers.

That year, I was looking for a date for the choir banquet. I called a guy I met through square dancing, who had initially annoyed me, but I developed a crush on him somewhere along the line. When I called, he gave some baloney about why he couldn't go, and in the background, I could hear his ten-year-old girlfriend (yep, he was sixteen, that should have said something in and of itself) giggling in the background. My self-esteem took yet another hit, but I ended up asking another guy from square dancing who I was pretty sure had a crush on me.

My Mom made my dress of course (I was still a year away from having a job and buying my own clothes). Jay was not bad-looking, just very quiet. That made it even more shocking when he brought me home and started pawing all over me. I managed to escape unscathed, and that pretty much killed that relationship.

My senior year was the only time I ever really got into trouble. It was pretty minor, and ultimately, it was my fault, not for the original crime, but my temper.

I have no idea why I was on the third floor that day. Besides the fact that I was (and am) about as anti-country as a girl raised in a Northern Texas town could be, there I was, dressed to the hilt in my western pants, shirt, belt, boots, and even a cowboy hat. It was pep rally day, and the theme was Western Day, and I was dressed for the part. I walked along an empty third-floor hall when my nemesis, Mr. Davis, entered the hallway.

He yelled at me, "Hey, it's against the dress code to wear a hat inside the school," or something to that effect. So, I took it off. I kept walking, and he stepped back into his classroom. I put my hat back on. He stepped back out into the hallway. Next thing I know, I'm being marched down three flights of stairs with a grip so tight on my arm it should have left a bruise. To the counselor's office, we went. Mrs. Jackson said to go to the pep rally and see her afterward. (I think I left my hat). I was so furious with Mr. Davis that I slammed her door on my way out.

I went to the pep rally and returned to her office as instructed. She looked at me and said, "I was willing to let the hat incident go, but you get three days detention for slamming my door." Guilty as charged. My biology teacher, Mr. Coffman, put in a good word for me but I still had to serve the three days of detention.

The worst part was that she also said I had to apologize to Mr. Davis. I climbed up to the third floor, and he was standing in the hallway conversing with the teacher whose classroom was next to his. I heard him say something about "troublemaker," and I knew he was talking about me. Which was the biggest crock of shit I had ever heard in my life. I swallowed my pride and my anger and apologized. I hope he's burning in Hell.

On a somewhat positive note, I had a crush on a guy who sat next to me in biology my sophomore year, Alan. He was dating a freshman at the time, but the next year, I was hanging out at school, and someone made a joke (I seemed to be the subject of a few jokes during my high school years,) and a bet was made. Something to do with the play that was going on, and if I won, Alan was supposed to take me out on a date. Well, I did win, but that would have ended that.

Except, I wrote him a long note about keeping bets, and he took me out. He was a perfect gentleman, and it was no Carrie experience. It was fun and romantic, and I maintained my crush on him even after we graduated.

Once I had my driver's license, I told our parents that I was going to the basketball games. Instead, I cruised Kemp Street like the cool kids and stopped at the gas station where Alan was working. He was always friendly, but we never officially dated. There was a rock station in Wichita Falls at the time (KTRN). I loved any song by The Eagles and "Cold As Ice" by Foreigner. Whenever "Best of My Love" came on the air, I would pretend I was singing to Alan. (Sound familiar?) Of course, who didn't love K.C. and The Sunshine Band? I still love listening to their music.

At least there were some bright spots throughout my life, not everything was demeaning and depressing. When Mom married Warren, we switched churches from Grant Street Methodist to another Methodist church closer to our new home. Attending church was not optional while I was living at home. My step-sister and I went to the high school Sunday school class. In that class was, of course, a pretentious snooty bitch named Biddy. I'm sure I was at the bottom of the scum pile in her eyes.

While attending that church, I attended a couple of young persons' retreats. I met a couple of cool people, one named Norma Jean (after Marilyn Monroe) and a guy named Ed. Ed was physically attractive enough, blonde and broad-shouldered. The three of us hit it off, but Ed and I also hit it off as a couple. Even though he lived about an hour from Wichita Falls, we maintained a long-distance relationship for a few months.

My Mom even allowed me to visit him and stay overnight with the guarantee from his mom that she would be chaperoning and I would sleep in a separate room, which I did. At any rate, one

Sunday, Biddy was going on about some blonde guy she had met at a youth retreat. I knew she was referring to Ed because she compared him to John Denver, whom he did sort of resemble. I can't even express the pleasure of informing her that we were seeing each other. She vehemently argued that we couldn't possibly be talking about the same guy. However, after comparing a few more pieces of information, her jaw dropped, and she realized we were. Score!

Ed started to talk vaguely about marriage and kids and such in a rather definite manner. I was barely a Senior in high school, not to mention there was something about his personality that I could not imagine being married to. I'm sure we shared some affection during our relationship, but we were not involved sexually. Eventually, I told him that I couldn't see him anymore. We did catch up a few years later, and I think he had married and had kids, adopted. He admitted he had imagined us getting married but it really was a moot point by then.

MAKING THE BREAK
(1976-1977)

I suffered through my senior year in high school in silence. I made a new best friend, Mary. She bought me the 45 of my favorite song at the time, "Carry On My Wayward Son" by Kansas. I stayed busy with school friends and activities. I bought my first car, a 1973 AMC Gremlin. I got my first job working in the kitchen at the Wichita Falls State Hospital, delivering meals to various wards. That's where I met my future first husband. He was a refugee from Vietnam, the same war my dad had been so determined to continue serving in.

Initially, it was Howard's brother that was interested in me. I was not attracted to him at all. Howard and I were frequently assigned together to serve food to the wards. We had a chance to get to know each other, and I thought he was good-looking. Eventually, he asked me out. We went to a movie, and I think I spilled popcorn all over his car. I decided I didn't want a serious relationship with him, so I didn't date him for a while afterward.

In the spring of my senior year, I thought I'd had enough of living with my "parents." One weekend, while they were out of town, I packed my AMC Gremlin with all my stuff and prepared to leave. I don't even remember where I was going. It didn't matter because my car died in the driveway, and I couldn't get it started. When my parents got home, Warren showed me the problem and how to fix it if it ever happened again. Go figure. I sucked it up for another two months.

Meanwhile, I was gathering my nerve to ask Alan to Senior Prom when I found out that my second-grade best friend had already asked him, not because they were romantically involved, but because they were really good friends. She was too nervous to ask the guy that she really wanted to.

I asked some other guys who had convenient excuses for declining my offer. One in particular told me he had already asked one of my best friends. He had, but she had turned him down. I should have gotten the message when I showed up once for a sock hop. I was waiting in the gym's foyer for who knows what when I heard a group of boys say something about how they were waiting for the REAL girls to show up. I guess if I could have made my nose grow a few inches and get swallowed by a whale, it would have qualified me as a REAL girl. Meanwhile, I just wore glasses and lived in a very middle-class home with a sexual pervert for a stepdad. Excuse me for disappointing you.

I was determined to go to prom, so as a last resort, I asked Howard. He agreed to go. We started dating regularly after that. About three weeks before graduation, I came down with mono. I had to quarantine at home during that period. It sucked because anyone with perfect attendance and acceptable grades was not required to take their finals. They made no exception that it wasn't my fault I got sick. I took all of my finals and passed with flying colors.

Meanwhile, I was stuck at home. Howard came to see me one day. Ironically, it was on the couch in the living room where I lost my virginity. Take that, Warren. Two days after graduating from high school, I moved out for good.

Initially, I moved in with my best friend, Mary. It only lasted two weeks, during which we would play Boston on an 8-track tape player of hers. One night, I had Howard over. The bedrooms didn't have doors, and I had put a sign outside the front door to knock before entering. She didn't take it well. We broke our lease, and the scummy landlord commented on my "Mexican" boyfriend. Discriminate much? He was a Vietnamese dumbass. I was lucky my mom knew an attorney who helped get us out of our lease.

HUSBAND #1
(1977-1979)

There was no way I was moving back home, so I convinced Howard to rent a duplex with me. He made me make all the phone calls, and I hated talking to people on the phone, and I still am not a phone person to this day. We found a place for $60 a month. I told the lady we were married, but I told her I had lied when I met her in person to sign the lease. She was very understanding.

I was so broke at one point that I didn't have gas money for a few days, so I walked to the State Hospital, which was about 4 miles away. I was still working in the kitchen so I was wearing all whites. Alan and his new girlfriend, a red-headed bitch named Sharon, passed me, and I could hear them laughing at me. Meanwhile, my well-intentioned mother put an insulated bag with steak in it in my (apparently unlocked) car.

The bag sat in the sweltering summer heat for a couple of days. We took that steak, stuck it in the freezer for a few weeks, and eventually thawed it back out and ate it. Somehow, we survived without any side effects.

Our neighbors on the other side of the duplex fought a lot. They ended up moving out, and we moved over. It was a little bigger, and it was only $75 a month. We had a little gas heater and a window air conditioner. We tried not to use the air conditioner, so the electric company was shocked when I contested our bill for being too high, which was super low.

When we were getting along we would play albums on Howard's stereo and sing along. Abba was common, Gerry Rafferty, Fleetwood Mac, and of course, The Eagles. Howard's favorite song was "Hotel California," which reminds me of him to this day.

We got married in January of 1978. He was the only man I'd ever been with sexually beyond kissing, and I was sure no one would want a "tainted" woman. It was a disaster. By now, we both were working as ward attendants. Ironically, I was on the bottom floor of a two-story ward which was men. Upstairs were women; from what I heard, that was even worse.

I met some interesting characters working on the ward. Floyd, who had been there for decades. His teeth had been pulled for biting another patient's ear off. At this point, he was pretty harmless, like the Abominable Snowman. He did like bopping me on the head while I was trying to get his tennis shoes on. Earl, who was in a wheelchair. He yelled a lot and would make himself puke. Jeff, who was still very young, had used some psychedelic drugs, and he was a chronic masturbator.

We had to pull him out of the bathroom for meals. My favorite was Fred. He had a huge crush on me. He had been studying for an Electrical Engineer degree and had a nervous breakdown. He was about 40 when I met him. He always had a cigarette dangling out of his mouth. My favorite Fred'ism is "Your cheatin' heart will tell on you. Sure as Shit."

There were other patients. One tried to strangle me with a belt. I think that was the same guy who tried to break the shatterproof office windows with a chair. One was Harry Krishna, and I would find him on his bed moving his penis without actually touching it. One guy had Parkinson's, and he would drop little balls of poop as he walked in his catatonic state. His wife came to see him regularly. The alcoholics would get hold of aftershave and drink it.

Two brothers came and went, Daniel and Michael. Michael called a cab once and, at the gate told them he was an attendant and he had an emergency he needed to leave for. They let him through but he came back eventually. Michael also had some of us sitting on the swing in front of the ward singing "Stairway To Heaven." I had a huge crush on Daniel. It caused me to make some bad decisions down the road.

In addition to the patients, the staff was also rather interesting. I was the youngest attendant by several years. There was a big, jolly black guy named George. There were three older ladies who had no doubt passed by now. They all smoked. If Irene sneezed once, she sneezed ten times or more. I was told that every sneeze makes your heart stop. According to an old diary I kept, my friend Nancy, who was one of the ward nurses, called me a few years later to tell me that Irene had died of a massive heart attack.

There was a guy a few years older than me. He was involved with one of the RNs who was several years older than him. I always got the feeling she didn't like me much. If she knew what happened between her boyfriend and me down the road she really wouldn't have liked me.

My favorite was Nancy. We went to see Midnight Run together which is still one of my favorite movies ever. To my husband's very strong disapproval I was hanging with new people and drinking beer for the first time in my life. I started with Red Draws (beer mixed with tomato juice); even though I hated tomato juice, it cut the beer taste, which took a long time to get acclimated to. (As an adult, I have grown quite fond of Bloody Marys even though I still hate regular tomato juice).

One night, Nancy, Jerry, and I went to see the Rocky Horror Picture Show, which had just been released in Wichita Falls. We wore cowboy boots and smuggled two beers each into the theater. No one knew anything about the movie yet so it was really quiet that first time through. Later, I went with my husband to see it, and you couldn't hear a word in the film because of all the shenanigans the audience was acting out. I think there are theaters still running the film today, 45 years later.

Eventually, the older women I worked with on the ward helped convince me that I needed to get a divorce. My husband told me that when I got so fat he couldn't stand it anymore, he would leave me. I wanted to go to school to study accounting, become a CPA, and minor in music piano. He told me I wasn't smart enough to be a CPA and I wasn't talented enough to be a professional pianist, but that I was smart enough to be a radiologist. I started the radiology program at Midwestern State University. I didn't do well with the hands-on classes and I knew it wasn't something I ever wanted to do. I had one Professor that I confided in, and he told me to stick it out so that I would have income until I found something I liked better. I just couldn't do it.

I think the final straw was the day I brought home a sweet dachshund puppy from a friend's house. Hung made me put her out on the porch for the night, and the poor thing whined all night. The next day, he told me the dog had to go. I ended up giving her to my former short-term roommate. I was tired of not being able to make any decisions for myself.

I told my husband I wanted a divorce. He moved back in with his parents. The last thing he said to me, looking at me through the screen door of our duplex, was, "You're not pretty, and you don't have a good personality. Men will only be after you for one thing."

Wait. You married an ugly, boring, and obviously stupid woman because…. You thought you were just going to run my life? Spoiler alert. I wasn't THAT stupid.

I'm now living in the duplex alone. I read the book "The Shining" by Stephen King and it freaked me out so much I had to put it in a different room so I could sleep.

I took a road trip in an ice storm to see the guy I had a crush on from the State Hospital, Daniel (one of those very bad decisions). We spent the night in a very cold hotel room where the heat didn't work, and nothing happened. I drove home the next day and got stranded on the highway. I hitched a ride with a van full of hippies and was lucky they were just normal people and just wanted to help me out. The next day, my co-worker Jerry drove me back to get my car.

Daniel and I actually wrote back and forth for a while. I even stopped in Mineral Point once and saw him again. There wasn't a chance anything was ever going to exist between us, but once I got attracted to someone, I had a really hard time letting go. I gave him my Choctaw pendant that all of the grandchildren had gotten from our grandparents. That is one thing I always regretted later. I was never able to replace it.

I gave my notice at the State Hospital, and Nancy threw a small party before I left; she, her husband Pete, George, Jerry, and me. I was drinking beer and T.J. Swanson. Despite Nancy's concern, I drove myself home. Jerry followed and pulled behind me in the driveway to my indescribable shock. He spent what was left of the night. We ended up having sex (he later confessed to cheating on his girlfriend, but to my knowledge, he never said with whom. Now you can imagine why she probably really wouldn't have liked me). Afterward, he wanted to take a shower with me but I was shy and turned him down, even though I had done it with Howard. Once again, even though it wasn't my decision to start something, I had a very hard time ending it. I don't recall being particularly attracted to Jerry prior to that night of the party, but I was nineteen. It was my second sexual encounter, and I realized that I was going to be completely alone for the first time in my life. Maybe Howard's prediction that men would only be after me for one thing held true in that case. I certainly would never understand why Jerry bothered with a cheap one-night stand unless he just wanted to see if he could do it. I went through a lot of tears and emotional turmoil while he went back to his girlfriend/fiancée as if nothing had happened. Eventually, I moved to Ft. Worth. Between Howard, Daniel, and Jerry, I found my perfect theme song, and I sing it at the top of my lungs sometimes still, "I Will Survive" by Gloria Gaynor.

According to my diary, I wrote many letters after my move to Ft. Worth, including to Nancy, Daniel, and even Jerry. I don't remember that and it's funny because I thought I always hated writing letters about as much as I hated making phone calls.

NEW BEGINNINGS
(1979-1982)

My first divorce was pretty simple. We didn't have kids or assets except for a car and a savings account. We had bought a newer car, which he kept and I took my Gremlin. We split the cash in half. We made (or rather, he made) several attempts to reconcile but I had reached the point of no return. The divorce was finalized, and we went to dinner afterward to celebrate.

I moved to Ft. Worth and stayed with my sister until I could secure a job and an apartment. It took about two months. My first job was at a nursing home, but I had no debt, and I was able to find an inexpensive apartment. Once again, Mom came through with a church friend who knew someone who knew the HR manager at Continental National Bank. I was hired as a part-time sorting clerk for about $3.75 an hour. It was enough to pay my bills.

About a month after I moved to Ft. Worth, Wichita Falls was hit by a devastating tornado. My whole life, I grew up with regular tornado warnings, but everyone said that Wichita Falls was too low-lying actually to get hit. Guess again. I drove back a couple of days later to check on things. Mom and Warren's house took a mild hit, losing a few shingles from the roof. A young couple we knew from church bought their house, having lost theirs altogether. Other people lost much more, including their lives. I found this excerpt on the internet: "45 people died in the Wichita Falls tornado. 25 of those deaths were vehicle-related. 16 of those 25 vehicle-related deaths were from people leaving their homes to escape the tornado. 11 of those 16 people's homes were untouched by the tornado." It was heartbreaking. After Mom and Warren sold their house, she got a job in Lubbock, and they moved there for a few years. I'm not exactly sure what Warren was doing; he was probably out terrifying young girls.

My first apartment was pretty bare. I slept on a cot at first until my grandparents somehow transported two single-mattress hide-a-beds that were super heavy. I had a hamster when I was in high school named Hamilton. I guess he died. I don't remember. He was so cute that I acquired a new hamster that I named Jeremiah. He died of pneumonia. One of his eyes had dried out and looked really weird, so I took him to the vet (yes, I did, in a little cardboard box). The vet gave me some medicine, but he died anyway. I even ended a date with him early so I could get back and give the poor thing his medicine. At least I tried.

Sometime after starting the job at the bank I got into an accident with the Gremlin. I ended up buying a used orange Honda Civic. It was a great car. At one point, the radiator overheated. I was able to get it somewhere (my apartment? I don't remember for sure) and pour water into the radiator. Except it wasn't the radiator. I poured pitchers of water into the oil sump by mistake. I finally decided that there must be enough water and drove the car. I drove it some way before it finally realized what had hit it and quit running. My boyfriend (coming up in the next section) and his brother flushed the oil sump several times with fresh oil and left it filled with new oil. They also put water in the radiator. They were both amazed when that Honda kept running for another two or three years.

My sister had joined a Baptist Church so I started going too. I really got involved; I joined the Singles class and met my first boyfriend since my divorce. It was doomed to fail since he wanted to be a Deacon (and actually became a minister, I believe), and the minister of this church was especially conservative. No matter what I did or how hard I tried, I was never going to be good enough to be the wife of a dedicated Southern Baptist. I read all the study material and visited church members in the hospital. I rode the bus that picked up kids for Sunday School and joined the choir. I even got fully immersed and baptized. I tithed 10% not of my net income but of my gross part-time income while I lived on hot dogs and Kraft macaroni and cheese. I was humiliated for my weight, and it wasn't really that bad. Another female member of the Single class gave me her "fat" clothes because she had lost weight. Thanks, Bitch. At least her boyfriend dumped her for a friend of mine in the church, and she ended up marrying a Methodist Minister. What comes around goes around.

I did get a kick out of a tubing trip that the Single's Class took. Brother Bass approved the trip as long as the girls wore shorts and shirts over their bathing suits (yes, seriously). But he couldn't control the fact that other female tubers didn't have tops on, and the guys in our group got their eyes full anyway.

I remember a few of us going to the movie "Animal House." I was the one with my hands over my eyes while my conservative Christian boyfriend laughed his ass off. I'm sure Brother Bass approved of that outing. He preached a whole sermon against B.J. Thomas for being a drug addict. You know, once an addict, always an addict. Once a sinner, always a sinner. Apparently, some of us are more sinners than others.

Lamar definitely had a sex drive. I assume he did his own laundry because he went through many tube socks while we were dating. He insisted we date other people but became jealous when I got dates and he didn't. During the summer, I decided to cover my hair while I was tanning and he told me I looked like a Mexican, and it wasn't meant to be a complement.

According to my diary, some of which I remember, most of it I don't, or very vaguely, I was balancing a lot of relationships during the two years after my divorce, John, who was a fanatical, but not unromantic, Christian maintenance guy for the Ft. Worth Water Gardens. It was a very cool and unique place. I loved going there when I was working downtown at the bank. There was Gaylon, who worked in the mail room at the bank and was very quiet. Neil, who I don't really remember, and another guy from church named Steve.

All (technically) platonic relationships. As it turns out, not one of them put any sexual advances on me, but neither did they really care about me as a person. They all tolerated my obsessive behavior to some extent, but over time, they all faded from my life for good. I can't say I'm sorry about that; I'm just sorry I wasted so much of my precious time on them. The next phase wasn't a whole lot better, just a different set of controlling, self-serving, manipulative men who, this time, were also willing to have sex with me.

Meanwhile, I tried picking up on college again by attending the University of Arlington in Texas. I took music theory, political science, and French. I hated political science and flat-out got an F. My French teacher was an absolute Bitch, but I had an A in the class, thanks to two years of high school French. I got a C in music theory. My car broke down the day I was supposed to take my French final. It was a bit of a drive from Ft. Worth to Arlington, and I had no transportation. I took an incomplete after working so hard to get an A.

After about two years, Lamar finally put our relationship to the test, and I failed. He asked God to approve financing for a ring, which was declined. The deal breaker was when the very conservative minister said he would marry us, but Lamar would never be able to serve in any capacity in the church. Trust me, God did me a huge favor on that one. The crazy thing was Brother Bass asked me who "cheated" first in my first marriage. When I said I thought my husband did, he asked me if I had proof. Like photos? What the hell kind of question was that?

To add insult to injury, Lamar told me at one point that another reason he couldn't marry me was because I hated kids. I had never really been around little kids besides my nephew and niece. I wasn't particularly comfortable around them at that point, but to say I hated them was a completely unfair assessment. Again, God saved me from a fate worse than death. Praise God and Hallelujah.

Lamar ended up dating and marrying the daughter of a minister. I was attending a church dinner one night, and one of the old cronies in the church was sitting at the table behind me, and I heard her comment, "I'm so glad Lamar found a NICE girl." Pretty sure she's been dead for a while. Good riddance.

In one last-ditch effort to fulfill God's will (according to the minister at the church), I contacted my ex-husband who was living in Houston by now. He came up for a weekend to see if we could reconcile. Then, I flew down to Houston and spent a weekend with him. That is when I really gave up on what the church expected of me. Howard would have given it another shot, but I realized we weren't together because we weren't right for each other. I felt bad getting his hopes up just to dash them once again, but I knew in my heart that I had to forge ahead alone.

Ironically, I had more dates and relationships during my "Baptist" phase than I had up to that point, and they were all platonic. Even though I was somewhat overweight and still wearing glasses and practically no makeup, Hung's prediction that men would be after me for one thing (sex) was not true at all. As it turned out, it wasn't until I got contacts, lost weight, and wore makeup that I seemed to attract the kind of men who would be after me for that "one thing."

FROM BAPTIST TO BARS
(1982-1984)

My job at the bank was a great change, and my redneck supervisor, Wanda, liked me and helped me a lot. I learned to operate a proof machine with my right hand because left-handed machines were pretty much nonexistent. I was pretty fast, too, next to a black girl who was crazy fast, and she was a bitch to boot. I even got promoted to day supervisor over one person. From there, I moved to the Transit department.

I trained a new girl, Mary. I should have been promoted to supervisor there, but I had a habit of pissing off upper management, so Mary got promoted over me. It was fine; she was pretty laid back, and we became really close friends over time. I wasn't mad at her, and it was a short shit with crooked teeth and glasses named Richard that had it in for me.

I became really good friends with one of the guys in the transit department, and that remained just a really good friendship until he moved to Austin. After some time, we lost touch. I think I blew it because I would call him late at night after I'd been drinking and cry on his shoulder. As much as he loved me, I think he finally got sick of it and stopped communicating with me.

I dated several other guys before I started dating the hot guy in the department, Chris. Okay, I had two or three "dates" with him. Everyone else thought he was so good-looking; I wasn't that impressed somehow, though we went out a few times. Yeah, me, the fat girl who still wore glasses. Then I told my supervisor friend Mary, and she told everyone else. Chris was lectured about his lack of taste. He was really interested in a fat blonde assistant to the President with big boobs who wore a lot of makeup and was married. No one had a problem with that.

I dated one guy in the Transit Department for quite a while before going out with Chris. He was short and stocky, but he had a very handsome face (in my opinion). On one of our first dates, if not our first, we went to a nightclub. I had never drunk hard liquor. That night, I was drinking Singapore Slings and Harvey

Wallbangers. Fortunately, I made it out to the sidewalk before I started puking my guts up.

Don introduced me to a rock radio station, 98 KZEW. They played Kansas, Foreigner, Styx, Van Halen, etc. I fell in love with that station. I had inherited a turn table in the divorce, so I bought all four of Foreigner's existing albums and one of Journey. Don flipped out and told me that kind of music was okay occasionally but that I was obsessed with it.

I found out that Don was seeing another girl from out of town. I even met her once. She was a heavyset blonde with her hair piled on her head in a bun. I don't remember her real name, but I began referring to her as Tweety Bird. Okay, not to her face, I'm not THAT mean! Don said he couldn't give her up because if he broke up with either of us, he would marry the other one. I hope he and Tweety Bird lived happily ever after because I was the one who broke up with him.

Chris got promoted to supervisor while I got my ass kicked out of operations. Richard (a short guy with crooked teeth) "strongly suggested" that I take a position in the bonds department or something along those lines in the main lobby. He said I would set an example for the other clerks that it was possible to move into a more prestigious bank area. The truth was he just wanted to get rid of me.

I hated it, and I asked to come back. They put me in the Research Department. My boss was a Latino bitch. I met my future best friend for life, Laurie.

Since I was disillusioned with the church and everything to do with it, I started going out with Laurie. I was very self-conscious since I was still wearing glasses, felt slightly overweight, and wasn't very adept at wearing makeup. I knew nothing about going to bars, so I mimicked everything Laurie did. We drank Special Export Light, Jack Daniels, and Coke and smoked Benson and Hedges menthol cigarettes.

We figured out that on our 15-minute breaks at work, we could smoke two cigarettes and have a Coke. One day I asked her why my smoke came out in big puffs and hers came out in a stream.

She said, "You have to inhale Laura." We went into the women's bathroom, and she showed me how to smoke a cigarette properly. Keep in mind I was twenty-three years old.

I was living in my own apartment and met a couple of guys. One was the maintenance guy for the complex, Tim. He was cute, and we screwed around for a while. Funny note: one day, Tim was folding his laundry. He was folding everything into tiny squares and putting them in his dresser. When I asked him why he was doing that, he said so he wouldn't have to iron them; sometimes, I still do that to this day.

Tim had a friend, and they really got me into smoking cigarettes. I also had my first hit of pot. Tim and his friend came over to my apartment with a bong. I had no idea what a bong was. They showed me how to use it, and I took a hit. I waited a minute and said, "I don't feel anything." I took another hit. I did not have contacts yet, so I was wearing my glasses on the couch. They told me to take my glasses off, stand up, and walk around a bit. Then it hit. On top of it, I was legally blind. They had a good laugh, but it kind of spooked me, and while I did smoke it again, it was never out of a bong, and I never really developed an attraction for it.

I met a guy named Mark. He was always wearing a hat, and one day, we all jumped in the pool, and he took his hat off. When he came up, I realized he was bald on top. He was a pothead and a little weird, but we both wrote poetry, and he was pretty nice to me.

I was trying to save money so I wasn't using the air conditioning even though it was a hundred degrees outside. Laurie and I would get ready to go out, and it was all we could do to keep our makeup from melting off as fast as we could put it on. Mark was so miserable he offered to pay my electric bill if I would turn the air on. I don't remember if he did or not.

While I was living in that apartment, Laurie, her sister Anne, and I decided to rent a house together. I hadn't given thirty days' notice on my apartment, so I typed up a note and told them I had kept a copy of it. They said it must have been lost in the changeover in management and did not penalize me for the short notice. (Ten Hail Mary's and Father Forgive Me. That probably isn't remotely the worst thing I've ever done in my life).

Eventually, I got "promoted" to cash ledger reconciliation, a third shift position. My little orange Honda Civic died, and I bought one of the only brand new cars I've ever owned in my life, a 1980-something stripped-down Mustang, beige with brown racing stripes. I didn't start the third shift until 11:00 so I drove to Dallas and partied before going to work. I scraped my new Mustang on the guard rail on each side on two separate occasions, driving back to Ft. Worth to go to work.

One night, I went into the women's restroom and fell asleep on the couch there. My supervisor was a really nice, very young man who gave me a warning. Anyone else probably would have fired me on the spot.

I was living with Laurie and Anne in our rental house. Our favorite hangout was a bar in Dallas called The Roxie. Laurie taught me how to play pool, and Anne taught me how to dance. Now, guys were looking at me in a way I'd never been looked at before. And now, being three or four guys away from being a virgin, I wasn't opposed to having sex with someone new.

Another night, Laurie and I had gone to the Roxie and it was early, so it was pretty empty. The DJ was a skinny black guy with big brown eyes. He came over to our table and handed me a rose. There was something about those eyes…

We kept returning to that bar, and I developed a relationship with Kevin. The first time we made love, I was more than a little intimidated because he was very dark-skinned, and it just seemed weird. I don't know why he continued to see me after I showed up at a party he had gone to, and I was so drunk that I had puked all over myself. I also don't know how I never got into an accident or got a DUI in those days, when more than once, I didn't remember driving myself back to Ft. Worth.

Kevin was also seeing a girl going to school in Nacogdoches so she wasn't around often. He was infatuated with her, but he said her parents would never accept her having a black boyfriend, so they were never going to have a future together. I suspect he was also seeing other women, and he had a crush on my roommate, my best friend's sister.

Kevin lived in the house the three of us girls rented for a while. I didn't realize it, but apparently, he also brought one of his other "girlfriends" over while I passed out in a drunken stupor.

I found out I was pregnant. Kevin basically told me he would not marry me or support me and the baby. I was spotting anyway, so I don't know if the pregnancy would have gone full term, but I decided to have an abortion. I had no money, so I called my Dad. His response was, "Why don't you ask your nigger boyfriend for the money?" I didn't speak to my Dad again before he died in 1991, about seven years later. Turns out my former boyfriend, bald-headed Mark, gave me the money and didn't even ask me to pay it back. The process was very simple and painless.

In a very short period of time, Kevin's "true love" also became pregnant, and because of her parents, she also had an abortion. Then the woman he'd been screwing in my house got pregnant. She must have stood her ground because he ended up marrying her. Funny, of the three of us, I consider her the least attractive and most lacking in personality. Maybe he saw in her what Hung originally saw in me, which, to this day, I can't even say exactly what that was.

I think it was after Kevin, but while I still had roommates, I had another experience smoking pot. We were sitting in the living room watching some goofy sitcom. It hit me way more funnier than it normally would have. At some point, we thought going to the Roxie was a great idea. It was a good 45 minutes from our house, so I had to stop and get gas. I pulled off of the highway and up to the pump. In those days, gas station attendants still put gas in their cars. The guy took my card and came back with what seemed like a boatload of paperwork. I had given him my Amoco card but I was at a Shell station that was right across the street. He told me I could use it, but I'd have to fill out all of the paperwork. I said, "Never mind, I'll just pay cash."

On another occasion, I got this brilliant idea to go alone to another bar we used to frequent in Ft. Worth. Try as I might the name escapes me now. This bar used to serve 3 for 1 drinks on Sunday nights. I would order a Colorado Bulldog, which would come in its mini pitcher. I don't remember if this night was a Sunday, but I know I was drinking. At one point, I was dancing with someone, and some other dancers were running into me. (Or is it possible I was running into them?) Let it suffice to say we were running into each other. I almost got into a fight with them over it. Maybe that's why, as I was leaving the bar for the night, I was one of two women and a handful of guys who were loaded up into a paddy wagon and arrested for public intoxication.

It probably didn't help my case that I nearly tripped going down the front steps. At the police station, I was put in a cell with several tough-looking black women. I kept banging on the bars and yelling to be let out, but there was a four-hour minimum detox period. When I was let out, I called my roommate Laurie to come get me. Like the best friend that she was, she showed up to pay my $50.00 bail fee. Unfortunately, all she had was her checkbook, and they only accepted cash. By a stroke of luck, a guy named John, probably the guy I had been dancing with, had also been picked up, and he paid our fines. Later, he asked me out, and as a show of gratitude, I dated him for a couple of months.

HUSBAND #2
(1984-1987)

True to my personality, I had a hard time letting go of Kevin. I dated other guys but never got very serious. Either they had no job, no sex appeal, or both. One guy would not tell me his age, and it turns out he was quite a bit older than me. He was an aspiring artist and would draw sketches of people to get us into private parties. He drew a really good sketch of me, but I haven't been able to find it in years. He got so broke that he paid someone to steal his Camaro. He almost screwed himself because he had missed an insurance payment but somehow managed to post-date it. He had a twelve-year-old daughter living out of state and ran out on me, leaving me with a $200 phone bill. At least he left me his bike and his art easel.

Then, I met the guy who would become my second husband. Ironically, I met him at The Roxy, where Kevin worked. He played pool. He had come to Dallas from Wisconsin to escape his fiancé, who had dumped him. He had gotten into a fight with her new boyfriend and was at risk of getting arrested. He was staying with two friends and one guy's girlfriend. I would stay over, and he would brag about his stereo system while we slept on the floor and the cats ran over us all night.

One night, I came to the house, and neither David nor Denise were there, so David's friend and roommate backed me into a corner and ~~hit~~ tried to put the move on me. Nothing happened, and I never said anything. I just made sure I was never alone with him again.

I was living in an apartment in Ft. Worth by myself. Against my better judgment, I quit my job, left my apartment, and moved to Spring Green, WI with David. I had three weeks of vacation and burned it up trying to get a job in Wisconsin. I took a position at a restaurant as a dishwasher and then a cleanup person at Burger King, both of which lasted about 3 days, and decided I was better off returning to Ft. Worth.

Meanwhile, I got my first taste of Wisconsin. I joked that every town had a bar on each corner. It was a bit of a culture shock to realize that the male population was not particularly into dancing. It was very common for the women to dance with each other. That was a huge difference from what I was used to, and it took me a long time to adjust to it. Eventually, I did because a lot of times David was the DJ, and if I wanted to dance, I didn't have a lot of options.

Initially, I left Wisconsin, intending to go back alone. But I ended up calling David halfway, and he met me on his motorcycle, and we went back to Ft. Worth together. This part is kind of fuzzy. Initially, I moved in with my cousin. But David and I had a fight, and he left. I located Kevin, and he came over one night and spent the night, even though he was with his unattractive, crazy girlfriend. He returned to her, and I got an apartment in my cousin's complex. I returned to the bank I worked for before leaving for Wisconsin.

Not long after, I found out I was pregnant. I met a really nice guy, not particularly good-looking, but he was really sweet and even willing to be the father of my baby. My conscience wouldn't let go and I found out David had moved to Florida, where his uncle lived in Venice, and I relentlessly pursued him until he agreed to come back to me in Ft. Worth.

He was a bit shocked as my sister, who was an aspiring beautician, had bleached my hair blonde. Not to mention, I was about 8 months pregnant by then.

My son was born on his due date, which was Mom's birthday, January 16th. I was in the apartment alone while David was hanging out with the people downstairs. I realized I was going into labor and called my friend Mary to confirm, but I had already eaten a can of Dinty Moore stew for dinner. Thankfully, David came back upstairs, and we went to the hospital. I was in hard labor for about 12 to 14 hours before the jerk I had for an obstetrician decided to show up. My water never broke, and I hadn't dilated past a four. They broke my water, and I still never dilated past a four.

Finally, my OB sent me down for X-rays. Turns out, after his snarky comment about my nice wide hips, my birth canal was too small. Especially since my son weighed 9 lbs. 2 oz, they prepped me for a C-section. When I told them I had eaten a can of stew they insisted on giving me Alka-Selzer before putting me under. I tried to tell them Alka-Selzer makes me sick, but they did it anyway. Sure enough, I vomited as I was going under and got pneumonia in my lungs. Now, not only did I have an incision, but the nurse would come in and put a pillow over it and tell me to cough to clear my lungs.

We didn't have health insurance, and the hospital wouldn't have admitted me except that we told them we were giving the baby up for adoption. We didn't know if we were having a boy or a girl. I ended up having a 9 lb. 2 oz boy. The adoption representative came to see me and told me she encouraged me to see my baby. She said if seeing him changed my mind about giving him up then I didn't have his best interests at heart to begin with.

So, the nurse brought in this beautiful baby boy with a head full of black hair and a complexion like a Choctaw, and I knew I could never let him go. Not to mention my grandparents adored him at first sight also. David and I were not getting along great, but this time, I knew I would figure it out somehow.

We were fortunate to get a Medicaid grant from the State of Texas that covered almost all medical bills. What was left was minimal enough that we could pay it off.

We're still living in an apartment in the complex that my cousin managed. It was a small one-bedroom apartment, barely big enough for the three of us. Then, my sister ran into financial trouble, and we agreed to take her and my niece, who was 10 years old. My sister offered to keep the apartment clean and cook, but the space was just too small, and it broke my heart to tell them they had to find someplace else to go.

I was off work for six weeks, but David had some sort of construction job and he needed a ride to work one morning, which was at max 15 minutes away. My son was sleeping in his crib so I drove David to work and came straight home. My son appeared to be still sleeping. The next thing I knew, I got a call from child welfare services saying I had been reported for child neglect. I knew it was my cousin, the apartment manager.

David and I met with child services, and they took one look at my son and said he's obviously healthy and well cared for. Which he was. I went down to the apartment my cousin lived in with her boyfriend, had him drag her out of the shower, and immediately started to try and pound the shit out of her. It took a lot to get past that, but eventually, we did for a while.

We stuck it out in Texas until summer, then hit the road for Wisconsin again. This time, I managed to get a job as a proof operator at a local bank, working the second shift. Initially, we stayed with David's parents and younger siblings until we could get settled. We ended up renting an apartment, which is still 38 years later, in one of the least desirable areas of Madison.

Comic note: When the drive-through at the bank closed each day I had to wait for them to turn in their transactions, which they did using the remote courier system. One day, I used the intercom and said something like, "Are you fixin' to close?"

Initially I got dead silence, and then I think someone replied, "What did you say?" I realized very early on that "Y'all" was a dead giveaway to my southern roots. Now I asked, "You mean I can't say fixin' either?" I still had a long way to go to become an acceptable Wisconsinite. To this day, I still have what I call a hybrid accent.

On Halloween, my co-worker babysat my son while David and I went downtown to State Street. It was pretty lame, and we walked around with our milk carton jug full of rum and coke without getting stopped or reprimanded. These days, Halloween on State Street is a huge event, charging admission, lines waiting to get into all of the bars, elaborate costumes, and no walking around with a jug full of liquor.

At this point in time, David was a welder for a local construction company. He also had a part-time business as a mobile DJ doing weddings, parties, and bars. I met a guy at one of the local bars he regularly DJ'd named Tom. He was good-looking enough, but mostly, he paid attention to me while David was working. We played pool, drank beer, and hung out. Then things went a little further, and I met him ~~on one~~ out one night when David wasn't working.

One night, I tried to get to him in Mazo from Spring Green in a heavy snowstorm. My car slid off the road. This was before the days of cell phones, so somehow, I must've hitched a ride the rest of the way into Mazo. I found him. He basically told me to go home. In the end, he really wasn't a nice guy. He divorced his wife and married some chic several years younger than him. It wasn't the last time I would see him, but a lot of changes happened in the meantime.

The first snowfall came in October that year and it was still snowing in February when we relocated again. David had an uncle in Venice, FL. This is how I remember the sequence of events. They are materially correct, if not 100% accurate. We took off in David's Dad's red station wagon. David's friend was looking for a change of pace, so he came down with us. We had to find a place to live, so in the interim, we were living out of the station wagon, which was also full of our worldly possessions.

I had nothing to do during the day, so I walked with my son, who is now about four months old, down to the beach for the day. The days in Florida that time of year are warm and the sun is very intense. I had my son protected, but I wasn't. At the end of the day I was burnt from my earlobes down to my little toes.

That night, we were parked in a prestigious neighborhood in front of someone's house. There was something wrong with the station wagon engine so the boys were working on repairing it. Somehow, a spark struck some leaked oil or fuel underneath the engine. The whole engine caught on fire. The homeowner came running out and was completely confused. When we told him to call the fire department, he just looked at us and said, "Things like this don't happen around here!"

Eventually, the fire department did show up. Even more miraculous were two women who lived together, stopping to see if we needed any help. They had both lost homes in fires. All of our clothing smelled like smoke. They packed us up and all our clothes and took us to their place. They washed the clothes about three times before making a dent in the smell. They gave me a bottle of vinegar for my sunburn. I don't remember much more except that their kindness and generosity will never be forgotten.

We found a house to rent but had to wait two weeks to move in. I'm sure the station wagon was toast, but I don't remember what we were driving then. Nor do I remember where Gary went for those two weeks. All I know is that we stayed in a campground for that period. David had a job and left me and my son in the campground all day. We had virtually nothing for food.

One day, I decided to walk with my son to the front of the campground to kill time. It was probably a mile and a half one way. No, David, so we turned around and walked back. Still no David and nothing for dinner. When he finally did show up, he said he had run out of gas. His co-worker had stopped to help him out, so he felt obligated to go out for a beer with him. I was so angry I could spit nails.

We finally got into our rental house. However, the utility deposits were expensive, so we didn't have electricity or water. David was resourceful enough to turn the water on from the main plumbing in the middle of the street. A couple of days later, he came home to a note telling him not to turn the water on again. He did, anyway. He was working and really couldn't get by without showering, even if it was in cold water.

As for me, I just wanted to watch the mini-series North and South with Patrick Swayze. We did have a TV but no electricity. We ran an extension cord over to our neighbor's outdoor outlet. They were really nice people, and I'm sure they wouldn't have cared if we had asked. It was only long enough to watch the show every night.

Eventually we got all of our utilities turned on. I got a job with a reinsurance company in Sarasota. I had to go through a physical exam, which included x-rays for TB. They asked me if there was any chance I was pregnant, and I suspected I was. I tested positive for a pregnancy test, but they hired me anyway, and I was covered by insurance. It was a great job, even though it was boring. I made some friends, and my manager was a super nice guy who gave me a Christmas candy bowl that I still have to this day.

I had an amazing GN, and she recommended an amniocentesis test because my protein test came back marginal to indicate the possibility of Down's syndrome. I was worried about the insurance, and I told her I wasn't going to terminate the pregnancy. The test was covered, and she said even if it was positive, I could prepare myself for caring for a child with Down's syndrome. It was pretty simple and painless. David was terrified of needles, so he almost passed out when they inserted the needle into my abdomen. I said it was not the length of the needle, but the diameter, and the needle was super thin.

They called me at work when the test results came in. First, she said the baby was healthy. Then she asked me if I wanted to know the sex. I said yes. When she said it was a girl, I screamed so loud the whole office could hear me. I got what I wanted: a boy first and then a girl.

Sometime in my seventh month, we decided to get married. We constantly fought to the point that my best friend didn't even come to the wedding because she wasn't sure we would go through with it. We got married on Siesta Key Beach, by a Justice of the Peace. I wore a dress Mom had made. Our guests were mostly co-workers, and everyone was dressed in shorts and T-shirts. Our entertainment was a beach bum who was juggling for donations.

The office threw me a baby shower; of course, it was all pink and frilly. They kept asking me, "Are you sure it's a girl?"

I worked up until the day I went into labor. Because of the trauma with my son, I was scheduled for a C-section. My due date was October 31st, so I picked October 29th for the surgery. We were at the grocery store on October 22nd, and I felt contractions. I looked at David and said, "I don't think we're going to finish grocery shopping."

At some point, we moved out of the rental house and into an apartment in Bradenton. We had made friends with our apartment neighbors, and they graciously took my son while we went to the hospital. Since I was scheduled for a C-section, they prepped me and took me in for surgery right away. I think my daughter was born around 11:00 p.m. I know it was a Wednesday because my son and daughter were all born on a Wednesday.

This delivery was so much easier than the first one. I wasn't in labor long, and I was conscious when my daughter was born. Her Dad gave me blow-by-blow details, which I could have done without, but when she cried, I teared up and said, "Is that my baby?" Well, of course it was, but I had to ask.

One day, I came home from work, and David answered the door. He had had a mustache ever since we met. When he answered the door, his mustache was gone. I freaked out. He looked so different I wouldn't let him touch me. I must have gotten over it eventually, but he looked like a completely different person.

I remember one night, my daughter wouldn't stop crying. We sat in a rocking chair and cried together. My Mom would have been there, but she planned her visit around my scheduled C-Section, and since I delivered a week early, I was on my own.

I don't have any strong memories of our life in Florida. I did go out a couple of times. I met a really scummy disc jockey at a bar there. I even went so far as to meet him at his apartment on my lunch break from work one day. I can hardly criticize anyone else's taste, and he was a total scumbag. I was just that unhappy. Little did I know how much worse it was going to get.

We stayed in Florida until my ten-year high school reunion in the summer of 1987. The plan was we would move to Texas. I went home for the reunion and David went to visit his family in Wisconsin.

I got a hotel in Wichita Falls and Mom tagged along to watch the kids. At the same time, I went to my reunion, which included a Friday night icebreaker, a picnic during the day on Saturday, and a dance on Saturday evening. My high school sweetheart from biology class and the one I had wanted to take to the Sweetheart Dance was at the bar Friday night. We chatted, but I had to get back to the hotel. We caught up again Saturday night and hooked up with another couple we had each been friends with in high school. After the dance, we all went out, and then I spent some time alone with Alan. I still had feelings for him.

Meanwhile, David got a job with a construction company in Wisconsin. He informed me that he wasn't coming to Texas and expected me to return to Wisconsin. I had an opportunity to stay where I was, but we were married. He was the father of my children, and I decided to try and make it work. I moved back to Wisconsin.

Once again, we moved in with his parents. There were no cell phones or, email or internet. I got a P.O. box, and Alan and I were writing to each other. Occasionally I called him from a pay phone.

I finally decided I needed to go back to Texas. David's Dad gave me an angry lecture about trying to leave the state with my children. I'm not sure why he cared so much; he and David's Mom were about the worst grandparents ever, especially compared to my family. I left the kids, my son now 2 years old and my daughter about 9 months, with David and his family. I took a week and drove down south. Initially, I met Alan in Wichita Falls, but by now he officially lived in Austin. I believe he cared for me, but he apparently understood the complications of my situation better than I did. He told me to go home and make my marriage work. If it didn't, he said, maybe I would meet someone else in Wisconsin. He went back to Austin, and I continued my solo vacation.

I visited friends in Ft. Worth with my Mom, who was now living in Lubbock with her pervert husband, and then I made the trek to Austin. I wasn't ready to give up on Alan quite yet.

I had his address from the letter writing we had done. He was pretty surprised to see me, but he was very gracious. That evening, we went downtown and listened to a live band. I spent the night at his apartment, where he lived with roommates. When he finally came to the bedroom, I remember sleeping on the floor for some reason, and we did have sex. It was literally quite anticlimactic and rather disappointing. I think it was at that point that I realized he was right. I needed to go back to Wisconsin and figure things out.

I was sad that in such a short time my daughter seemed to have forgotten me already. We recovered, and the four of us moved into a little rental house on the west side of Madison that was part of a complex of identical houses.

I was unemployed for a few months and stayed home with the kids. I adore my children, but I was not cut out to be a domestic homemaker. David and I had started to fight. One day, I chased him down the sidewalk with a frying pan. I became involved with the maintenance guy. We would have a little afternoon delight while the kids were napping. He introduced me to the concept of a vibrator. He also told me that David and I were known in the neighborhood as "The Fighters." A foreshadowing of things to come.

LIFE AT RURAL INSURANCE
(1987-1996)

I managed to get a job as a New Business Clerk in the Group Health Department of Rural Insurance. I remember going to the interview on the back of David's motorcycle dressed in a skirt and hosiery. He stopped a little too hard at a stop light, and I fell off the bike. I was a little shaken up, but I got the job anyway.

There were two of us that were hired in that department and we started on the same day. Our manager was better than some, but still, your typical anal boss, and she couldn't pass up an opportunity to make corrections on anything she reviewed.

I became friends with another young woman in the department, Diane, as well as Carol, the one who started the same day I did. We were all close in age.

Diane ended up getting promoted to supervisor. I ended up getting promoted to Group Lead, where the other processors could turn to for questions and assistance. It turns out that our manager thought Carol would be her star employee. She was lazy and called in sick all the time. I worked my butt off, and while I still didn't suck up to management, my efforts were recognized for probably the last time in my career.

Diane had a guest pass to Elaine Powers, a popular health club at the time. I went just long enough to get motivated to lose my baby fat from my pregnancy with my daughter. Thanks to my OCD, I lost a lot of weight and got down to 110 pounds, which I hadn't weighed since 6th grade.

The company implemented a Health and Wellness program. They brought in consultants who weighed and measured us and offered an incentive program where we broke into teams. The team who lost the most weight over a given period of time got a reward. Diane and Carol thought I was the ideal teammate since I seemed to be so successful at losing weight. Except, I didn't have any more weight to lose, even though my super skinny, flat-chested consultant told me I only had three more pounds to lose to reach my ideal weight and body fat goal. I was so skinny you could see my neckbone and ribs. I was so discouraged that I started gaining weight again.

We had moved into an apartment, but the housing market was very lucrative, so we decided to buy a house. David was working with a lender, and we applied for a VA loan, which offered an eight percent interest rate that was considered desirable at that time. We had to jump through many hoops, and David was constantly on the phone with the lender. He went back and forth; one minute, our income was too high, then our expenses were too low. One of the last calls he made, I was in the background screaming, "Tell him to make up his mind!" That was probably one of the nicest things I was screaming. Ultimately, we got the loan.

We bought a little house on the west side that was dated but in overall good shape. It was close to a grade school, in between two parks and convenient to my work. David was pretty handy and did much work on the house to bring it up to more modern standards.

David was still working his construction job, but he was also DJ'ing on the side, and business was picking up. One day, he came home and told me he wanted to quit construction and make DJ'ing his full-time job. I didn't have much to say about it; I knew he hated construction and was a very good DJ. The problem was his schedule went from a regular weekday job to working nights and pretty much every Saturday night. His business grew enough that he hired other guys to take on additional gigs. He bought a couple of used vans to haul equipment.

It seems like this is when our relationship really started to fall apart. We were working completely opposite schedules, and except for essential expenses, he was investing his DJ income back into the business. We started fighting a lot, and money was a major issue. The house was always a mess, and the kitchen was usually piled high with dirty dishes.

We had found a sitter for the kids since they weren't in school yet. One day I got a call at work that I needed to come get the kids right away, no explanation. It turns out the sitter's eleven-month-old son, whose birthday was the same as mine, had strangled himself on a diaper stacker attached to his crib. It was February, and the ground was frozen, so they stored the body until late spring when the ground thawed out. That poor couple had to identify the body again to make sure they had the right one. It was very tragic all the way around. Meanwhile, we had to find a new sitter.

Our neighbor across the street started watching the kids. Her husband was a little strange, and he was always into everybody's business. At one point, when his wife and my husband were away, he even hit on me. It was disgusting. However, our sex life was in the toilet. David would bribe me by offering to buy me new clothes or some other "reward," which made me feel like a prostitute. At times, I would have tears running down my face during sex. He told me if he ever went two weeks without it he would go find someone else. He would not get a divorce, just find someone who was more cooperative.

One day, I was folding laundry in my daughter's bedroom. I was crying again. My three-year-old looked at me and said,

"Mom, I think you should find a Dad who doesn't make you cry anymore." Out of the mouths of babes.

I wanted to leave, but if I brought it up, David would threaten that I would never see my kids again. Somewhere in the logical part of my brain, I must have known that was never going to happen. I didn't really have anywhere to go or the means to support myself, so I just stayed and remained miserable. At one point, I remember going through the house with a paper bag and collecting every medication I could get my hands on. Again, I knew there was nothing there that would kill me, more likely just make me really sick or, worse, cause permanent brain damage. So I sat on the floor with my bag full of drugs and cried. I convinced myself that if I just went to sleep, things would look better in the morning. I was right.

I became a wino. When David was working and the kids were sleeping, I was drinking and doing workouts in the living room. I was also still smoking when I thought I could get away with it, even though David professed to detest it.

The insurance company decided to install new computer software for the Group Health line of business, but they needed to organize a team to do the initial testing before we could go live. I was chosen to represent the new business staff. Other members comprised upper management, claims, and information technology (IT).

It felt like there weren't enough computers for everyone to have their own, so we usually worked in pairs. I remember being paired with a guy from IT. He was a little older than me, fourteen years to be exact, but he was funny, and we got along really well, so it made the training a little less mundane.

On June 10, 1990, my maternal grandfather passed away. He had been struggling with Alzheimer's and bone cancer that developed after he had prostate surgery. He was the closest thing to a real Dad I ever had, and nothing was going to stop me from going to his funeral. It didn't prevent David from trying.

He argued that we didn't have the money, but he always managed to come up with money when he wanted something. I don't remember exactly how, but we did come up with money after more arguments and fights, and I did make it down to Oklahoma for the funeral. It was unfortunate that, at that time, it was common for companies to offer only one day of funeral leave beyond parents, siblings, and children. I used vacation time to make up the other days I was gone.

When I returned to work, I had a very sweet sympathy card waiting for me from Joe, the IT guy. It was a refreshing change from the shit I got from my husband. I had been going for walks on my lunch breaks and now Joe asked if I would mind if he joined me.

Joe wasn't exactly Cary Grant, but he was funny, and I wasn't used to getting attention from men who had a college education and wore a suit to work. I was still fairly thin, and my hair was frosted. Despite the fourteen-year age difference, we got along really well, and our relationship developed into something more than just friends.

I don't remember the exact circumstances, but I was alone with Joe in his cube at work. He surprised me with a peck on the lips. I was a little surprised but not at all offended. He got to work pretty early before anyone else was in his building, so I started hanging out with him early for a while.

Another big reason that we related so well was that I was married to a jealous, obsessive, controlling husband, and he was married to a psycho wife. Apparently, she would just go off on screaming rants, and they hadn't had sex in years.

I think Joe really believed he would have the strength to ~~live with~~ leave his wife. However, they had a juvenile son and Joe was a devout Catholic. It didn't help that David suspected something or got a tip from someone and met us on the front steps as we were leaving for our walk. I don't remember what was said, but it was enough to cause Joe to be intimidated by David. Despite that, we maintained our relationship.

Joe was going on a short business trip to Chicago, I think, and we worked out the details so that I could go with him. He had a business suite so I stayed in the bedroom while he had his meeting with his business associates in the living room. That night, we went out and we both got so drunk we barely found the hotel room when we got back.

The trip was not over for him, but the next morning, he got a call from someone who was looking for me. Joe panicked and put me on the first bus back to Madison. Apparently, the word got around, and we were the gossip subject of the day.

At one point, Joe had told me that when I was ready to leave David, just let him know and he would leave his wife. But when David and I had a big fight, I called Joe, and he met me kind of like Alan, only worse. I think he was realizing that it was much more complicated than that.

Of course, none of this was improving my relationship with David. One night, we were in the car, and David was driving. The subject of the kids came up, and I got the usual threats about making sure I never saw them again. I think I was trying to jump out of the car when I leaned over and bit David on the shoulder hard enough to leave teeth marks for a while.

One of the times I was trying to take off, my car wouldn't start. David had pulled the coil wire. So, I jumped on my bicycle and took off anyway.

I don't know what finally changed, but I did end up moving out of the house. I sublet an apartment not too far from our house. I had minimal furnishings but I did have a television, and yes, I did have the kids part-time.

I don't remember the exact dates, but I know it was getting into winter when I sublet that apartment, sometime around December 1990. I think it was February when we got a monstrous snowstorm. They closed the office, which was good because my parking lot was so deep in snow that I couldn't get out. I ended up calling David.

I had been keeping journals for some time, and I think I had three. When David came to help me get my car out, I gave him all my keys. Unbeknownst to me, he had a spare key made for my apartment. I didn't keep my journals hidden, and he took them. Once again, he threatened to use them in court to take my kids away from me. When I did get them back, eventually, I threw them out, unfortunately, because they could have been helpful in writing this part of my story.

The computer system for Group Health never went live. They ended up selling that line of business altogether. Since I wasn't in a position to go back to school, I started some self-study insurance courses. I was hoping to get a position as an underwriter apprentice. Unlike my sister and step-sister, I was not content to stay at the bottom of the job pool. I was more like my mother, determined to escape a bad situation. Turns out the underwriter position was rigged and filled by a friend of one of the senior underwriters. I stuck with it anyway, ten courses over five years. The payoff came a few years later, but that's part of my other story.

I still had a goal of becoming an accountant, so I applied for an accounts payable clerk position in accounting. Finally, a positive break. It was a life changer when I got it.

When the sublease on the apartment ran out, I moved back into the house. On March 12, 1991, my dad passed away from liver damage at the age of 64. I didn't go to the funeral because I hadn't spoken to him in years. If I had it to do over, I would. He had a military funeral, which would have been cool to see, and I didn't realize how upset my sister was about his death. I would've been there for her. Ironically, I got three days of funeral leave and flowers from the company. It would have made more sense for my grandfather.

I didn't stay in the house long and ended up renting a townhouse centrally located to the house, work, and the kid's school. By now, I think my daughter was in kindergarten, and my son was in second grade.

The crazy thing about Joe was we never technically had sex. He experienced premature ejaculation every time we tried. He was very good with me, but he was depressed and disappointed that he couldn't control himself.

David was dating other people even though he relentlessly pursued me whenever he got the chance. I think it was his girlfriend Teresa that persuaded him to get a divorce. At any rate, in June of 1991, we were legally divorced.

Teresa was some sort of executive at Cuna Mutual. David would throw in my face that she read to the kids every night they were there. Well, so did I, and they were with me a lot more often. Besides, I was at every musical, every play, every concert every teacher's conference, every sports event. I heard that one time my daughter said to her, "You have a big nose. Kind of like a witch or something." OMG, I laughed my ass off.

My car broke down, and in spite of our differences, David loaned me one of his vans. The next morning, I woke up to a vulgar message in dark red lipstick written on the windshield. Apparently, Teresa thought David had spent the night. If you think I was crazy, I think she was one up on me.

David went with me to look at a car. It was a privately owned Cutlass Sierra. We had the kids and while we were looking at the car, my daughter was following their Dalmation around. No one noticed the dog went into its kennel, and my daughter tried to follow it. The dog jumped and bit her on the cheek. We heard the scream and saw the blood running down her face. We took her to the emergency room. They didn't stitch it because they didn't want to seal dog germs in her face, so they just put a butterfly patch on her cheek. She still has a small scar, but if you didn't know better, it looks like a small dimple.

I was still "seeing" Joe, even though it was pretty clear we weren't going anywhere at this point. Then he informed me that they were moving to Florida. It was at the same time a co-worker told me she was leaving the company. There was a going away party for her, and I was drinking gin gimlets or maybe vodka. Either way, I got very drunk and very emotional, and she said, "I didn't realize you were going to miss me so much." It wasn't about her, and it was about Joe.

I drove home, miraculously without incident. However, when I got up the next morning, my car was parked crookedly, and my driver's side door was open. It wouldn't be the first or the last time I wondered what God was saving me for. While I don't believe in organized religion, I do believe there is a higher power that kept saving my ass for some unknown reason.

The first year I was in the townhouse, I took a part-time position at J.C. Penney's over the Christmas shopping season. I was put in the men's department. Of course, I had to structure my hours around my time with the kids. Somehow, I ended up meeting a dark-haired Irish guy around my age who worked in the shoe department. I had no idea what I was getting myself into.

Patrick and I started dating. Then I found out he was living in low-income housing, he had an agent who managed his money, and he was an alcoholic. He took medication that would make him sick when he drank, but he knew when his monthly distribution of funds was coming in, so he would go off of the meds a few days before. When he got his money, he would spend it on alcohol and go on a bender until the money ran out. It was unfortunate because he was a really nice person when he was sober. He was a complete ass when he was drinking.

Patrick did one really cool thing while we were dating. My grandmother was having a "surprise" 80th birthday party in Oklahoma, and of course, I wanted the kids and me to be there. I booked flights with Midwest Airlines, which was a premier airline back in its day, and the tickets were not inexpensive. I could only afford them because I hadn't maxed out my credit card at that point. I don't remember for sure, but I think it was United Airlines that started advertising discounted flights which were significantly less than the ones I had already booked. The problem was my tickets were non-refundable, with no exceptions. Patrick picked up the phone and called Midwest Airlines. He gave them a big sob story, at least most of which was true, about how I was a single mother on a limited income and could use all the breaks I could get. By the time it was said and done, I got a full refund and booked the flights with the other airline.

It took a while, but I broke up with Patrick. I felt bad for him, but I wasn't his mother, and I couldn't handle his drinking binges anymore. I had already noticed a guy a few doors down from me who appeared to be single and not bad-looking. His name was Tom. Gradually, I would catch him going back and forth to and from his apartment and start a conversation. Eventually we did end up dating for a while. As was my luck, though, he was obsessed with his ex-wife, who was living in Canada at this point. She was the only woman he had had sex with, and he was clinging tightly to his not-quite virginity. He drove me crazy because he would do everything, but he wouldn't do that. (Get it?)

One day, I was inside the townhouse, and I mistakenly let the kids, who were now around eight and six years old, if that, go outside alone. Some moron at the convenience store around the corner gave them a book of matches. They decided to build a campfire in a clump of pine trees outside the front of the complex. Things got out of control, and the next thing I know I'm answering the door to a couple of burly firemen. They extinguished the fire, and the kids were unharmed. I definitely wasn't up for any Mother of the Year awards at this point.

On the other hand, they were riding their bikes around the block when the tornado sirens started going off. I immediately went to look for them but we kept missing each other initially. I found them and my neighbor's 12-year-old daughter with her cat and we all stayed in the townhouse until the danger had passed.

The last time I saw Joe in person, I flew down to Florida. His wife was out of town visiting her mother or something. He agreed to let me come down. It was pretty uneventful in every aspect. I have a picture of me in a bathing suit, sitting on the beach, smoking a cigarette. I had put on quite a bit of weight. I'm sure everything put together had put an end to any delusions of Joe and I ever ending up together. The weight, the smoking, the poor housekeeping on my part, my depression, an intimidating now ex-spouse, the lack of sexual satisfaction, a guilty conscience. The distance was just the final straw. It took some time for me to look back and admit that we would not have been a good match. As much as I try to ignore religion, something in the universe has a better plan waiting for me. I just didn't know it yet.

While I was in the townhouse for three years total, despite depression, drinking, and smoking, I continued my self-study insurance courses. I also signed up for a writing course to write children's books. I had always wanted to be a writer, I knew I had a talent for it, but that wasn't the direction I wanted to go, so I paid for the course but never finished it.

I completed the ten courses for the Life Office Management Association and earned my FLMI (Fellow Life Member of the Institute) in September 1993. It was the last year that the insurance company sponsored a graduate to the national convention, which was in Toronto that year. I tried to convince Tom to go with me and even told him he could try contacting his ex-wife. In the end, he turned me down.

As crazy as it is, I ended up taking my ex-husband. In between his other girlfriends, he was still pursuing me. The trip went fine. The only thing that stands out in my mind is having a chocolate-covered pear for dessert at dinner. It did not "pair" well with the wine I was drinking, and I got rather ill.

When my lease was up in the third year, I moved back into the house with David. I had been promoted to the Finance department. The job description required an associate's degree in accounting, which I didn't have. However, I had a working relationship with the two senior accountants in the department, and they requested me over another candidate who was a rather obnoxious woman with all of the requirements. They had a working relationship with her also and I won out.

I stayed in the house for about two years. During that time, I gained accounting experience in the finance department, even though our manager was not the easiest person to get along with. The VP was even worse. The whole company was expected to fill out these weekly time management reports, where you kept track of the volume of things you did. Most of the things we did fell into the "Other" category, and it felt like a huge waste of my time. I decided not to fill it out anymore. When I had my review with the

VP, who was a female lesbian, all she said was she was going to put a note in my file. I didn't get fired or demoted so I could live with that and no more pointless reporting.

It was an interesting two years. I didn't really want to be in the house, but I had acquired several thousand dollars in debt and was tired of David's relentless advances and not being with my kids all the time.

The first year after I moved in, I bought a little camper that was attached to the back half of a van that had been cut off to accommodate it. I was able to take two weeks off on vacation that summer, and we went out west to Mt. Rushmore, Yellowstone, Jackson Hole, where we went white water rafting down the Snake River, and Glacier National Park.

We saw a ton of animals, had a lot of adventures, and the kids had a great time. My favorite story is at Jackson Hole (I believe). We parked the camper and hiked a trail into a very scenic spot where you could climb up some cliffs and get a spectacular view. When we came back down the kids and I got separated from their

Dad. I got confused and didn't realize the trail went out on the other side in the opposite direction from where we were parked. We had no water or snacks. I tripped over a rock, and my knee was bleeding. I started crying. Then, we came upon a group of tourists who had stopped dead in their tracks to stare at something. It was a "baby" bear several yards away in the grass, munching on the vegetation. Now, in 1995, I had a Kodak-style camera that used film. I tried to snap a shot, but it was the end of the roll of film and it automatically began to rewind. I held my breath as I waited for the bear to hear the noise and change course to eat me for lunch instead.

Thankfully, he didn't, but I didn't get a picture either. Eventually, we made our way to the end of the trail, and a park ranger gave us a ride to the other side, where the camper was parked and David was anxiously waiting. His goal had been to see a bear and he missed it. I got a certain sense of satisfaction out of that.

The following summer, I took two weeks of vacation again. This time, we headed for Canada. We went back to Toronto, then Montreal and Quebec. We came home through New York and New Jersey, where David's brother was living at the time.

During those two years my daughter was able to take dance and a few horseback riding lessons. My son took karate and played soccer. David bought a beautiful metallic blue Firebird that I drove on occasion. The license plate was 1HOTFB, meaning One Hot Firebird, but apparently, interpretation depended on the individual reading it, especially when I was the one driving it.

I ended up buying a brand new deep purple Saturn, against David's wishes, but since we were legally divorced, he couldn't really stop me. Even in my dire financial circumstances, I somehow got the financing.

Other than the vacations, though, tension was still high. David had to review every check I wrote to make sure I was paying legitimate bills. We were still fighting. One night, I grabbed the closest thing I could find, which was a gallon of milk from the fridge, and tried to pour it over his head.

MOVING ON
(1996)

After eight years and three departments at the insurance company, I decided it was time for a change. I started interviewing for accounting positions with other businesses. I now had experience but I didn't have a formal education in accounting. I was getting interviews but no job offers. I added an Associate's Degree in accounting to my resume. I interviewed for an accounting assistant position with a small print and mail company at the same time, I interviewed with a battery company and a travel agency. The travel agency was the first to make an offer. It wasn't a great offer, but I really wanted to leave the insurance company, so I took it.

Meanwhile, the battery company wanted to check my references (where I got my associate's degree). I told them I had accepted another offer, so it no longer mattered. I started the job with the travel agency. Their equipment was really outdated, and the environment wasn't particularly appealing. On about my third day there I got a call from the operations manager with the print and mail company. I had met with both him and the owner, and I had also met with him ~~on one~~ individually. Not only was the pay and opportunity significantly better, but he was extremely attractive and seemed pretty easygoing. It was a no-brainer. I accepted the offer and gave my notice to the travel agency right away. When I asked Ed what I should wear, he told me whatever I had worn to the interviews was fine.

Officially, I reported to the owner of the company, but in reality, I dealt much more closely with Ed and the owner's wife, who worked part-time and handled more complex aspects of the accounting side. Of course, initially, I didn't know anything about Ed, like age, marital status, etc. I stumbled across something in a filing cabinet that revealed his birthday. He was eleven years older than me, but you never would have guessed it. At about five foot eight, with blonde hair and blue eyes, very athletic and well built, he looked especially good for his age. (I was 37 at the time, he was

48). Later, I found out he was in the last stages of finalizing a divorce.

The company had a sales staff of four that I can remember offhand, of varying ages and personalities. When I came to work each day, I noticed a black Nissan 300ZX in the parking lot. I decided it must belong to the one salesman who was about my age, very outgoing and quite a character. Turns out the car belonged to my hot boss as I watched him get in leaving for lunch one day. At this point, star-struck doesn't even begin to describe it.

I hadn't had much reason to care about my appearance at the insurance company. Now David noticed that I was wearing makeup to work every day. I was still smoking, but not at work.

I decided to make a bold move, and I offered Ed a proposition. I told him that if he took me to lunch in his Z, I would take him to my Saturn. He took me up on the first part of the bargain. He kept stalling on the second part. When I would ask him when we were going to lunch in my car, he just said "We will." Finally, I walked into his office one day and made him put it on his calendar. We had a date.

I noticed many of the warehouse workers, especially the busybody receptionist, did not like Ed very much. On Thursday night, we had a company happy hour. It was a small group, and Ed came, but he left early. I took the opportunity to ask the owner's wife, who was a super sweet individual, why everyone complained about Ed. She didn't really have an answer either. From what I could see, he mostly expected people to be there when they were supposed to and do their jobs while they were there. I guess that was asking too much.

I got very intoxicated at that happy hour. I attempted to drive home and got fairly close, but I pulled into an empty parking lot and fell asleep. When I did get home in time to get to work that day, David was suspicious of my whereabouts. Well, that's my story, and I'm sticking to it. Fortunately, I knew Ed was out of the office that Friday, so I didn't put as much effort into my appearance and I wore my glasses instead of my contacts. It was a long day, but at least it was Friday.

One day, I had been on the phone with David. I'm not sure what we were talking about, something involving the kids as usual, and I was crying. Ed walked by my cube and asked me what was wrong. I tearfully told him I had an argument with my ex about the kids, and he said, "We need to talk." I didn't know it at the time but he had dealt with the same kind of situation with his first wife, his kids' mom. I told him I was planning on moving out and he said when I did, then we could have a conversation. He told me many times that he believed you should end one relationship before starting another.

It was obvious things were not going to work out with me and David. Once again, I had to make the difficult decision to move out and not be with my kids one hundred percent of the time. Before that happened, there was one last incident that cemented our separation. It happened one evening when David wasn't home. We acquired a piano after we bought the house, which I had taken to the townhouse. Now, it was sitting in the garage along with David's classic Trans Am. I was depressed and drinking as usual. I went to the garage to play the piano and drowned my sorrow. I did not have any ill intent in mind when I went out there. I can't even explain what happened, but something inside me snapped. I took a couple of tools off the garage wall. I used one to puncture all four of the tires on the car. I used the other one to put scratches in the paint on both sides. Apparently, I had been suppressing some pretty intense anger, and it blew up like a hand grenade.

I didn't tell David what I did. He found the car himself and knew I had to be the one who did it. I stood my ground and refused to confess. It wasn't until he called the police and they came to investigate that I had to spill my guts. Ultimately, David told the police that he didn't want to press charges. They told him it wasn't his decision anymore. Months went by before I had my court date. I met one-on-one with some woman from the courts. Initially, I was charged with criminal damage to propertwhich is a felony. Since I had moved out by then and David and I were not sharing the same space, I convinced her that it was a one-time domestic dispute, and she lessened the charge to county disorderly conduct, which was a misdemeanor. I have a message to all the girls out there who listen to the Carrie Underwood song "Before He Cheats," Don't Do It!

Meanwhile, before my court date came around, I did move out again. I found an efficiency apartment between the house and work. I got a futon to sleep on, which the kids used when they were there, and I think I slept on the floor. I brought our Shih Tzu puppy, Smudge, with me, which was a disaster. He was not housebroken and he shredded every piece of material he could get his teeth into. I ended up giving him away, but not before the apartment looked like a total garbage dump, and it stayed that way until I moved out.

I took a part-time job as a night auditor at a hotel. It was very short-lived. It meant leaving the kids in the apartment alone on the nights they were there and I was working. It wasn't the worst neighborhood, but it wasn't great. Besides, working the third shift on the weekends and working a day job during the week wasn't "working" out very well to begin with.

True to his word, we scheduled a date once I told Ed that I had moved out of the house. I was still smoking, but I knew he wouldn't date a woman who smoked. One week before our date, Sunday, September 8, 1996, I smoked my last cigarette. I didn't smoke again for almost four years. That is part of the second half of my story.

One week later, Sunday, September 15, we had our first official date. I will describe as much as I can remember, although I will skip over some details that I'm not completely sure about and are not critical. The first thing I remember was going to UW Memorial Union. We ordered a pitcher of beer and sat outside on their large outdoor patio. The bees were ferocious, and they kept swarming around my head, so Ed kept swatting them away from me. Just that simple thing got me right in the heart. (Sigh) We took a walk down a path off of the patio area and had a serious conversation about how he had been hurt in his previous two marriages, and I promised him that I would never hurt him. He also said, "And if you're thinking of having more children, I am not the man for you." Okay, he's 48, I'm 37. He had a 22-year-old daughter and an 18-year-old son, and I had an 11-year-old son and an 8-year-old daughter. He'd had a vasectomy, I had a tubal ligation, and I was on birth control to minimize the distress that came with my monthly cycles. Problem solved. After the union, we went to a small, locally-owned Mexican restaurant called Pasqual's. It was the perfect date so far.

I must have driven to Ed's house or met him and followed him home. One detail I'm not really sure about. Either way we both ended up at his house, which he just recently purchased. He hadn't even received the furniture he had ordered for the living room. It was unfortunate that he had moved out of his house on the west side of Madison, close to work and close to my apartment, and bought a house on the far east side. At least it was Madison, not Chicago, so it could have been worse.

We walked into his kitchen, and that's when we kissed. We didn't stop kissing until we left a trail of clothing on the way to the bedroom and ended up in bed. I would like to tell his subordinates that all the jokes they had made about him being impotent were entirely false. I don't know about fireworks per se, but it was definitely an enjoyable experience.

I didn't spend the night and went home to my tiny apartment. The next day was Monday so I got up and got dressed for work as usual. I got there and sat in my cube. Shortly after I went to Ed's office, for whatever reason, he was sitting at his desk staring at the wall as if in a coma or something. I started to panic. I knew he was asking himself what the hell happened and how he could have a relationship with a woman who reported to him. I asked him if he was okay. I don't think he was quite yet. I thought that might be the end of it. In fact, it was just the beginning. That is the second half of my story.

What took place over the next twenty-seven years is nothing short of a miracle. I know I have a lot of work to do to tell the rest of my story, but it is just as important as the first part. A story of love, adventure, challenges, tragedy, and heartache. I hope that you found this book inspiring, and I hope that you will still be here when I pick up where I left off. Stay tuned.